Mystery of Leaves

A silence, a cross-road and a journey begins

Mystery of Leaves

A silence, a cross-road and a journey begins

Prasanta Behera

BLACK EAGLE BOOKS
2020

USA address:
7464 Wisdom Lane
Dublin, OH 43016

India address:
E/312, Trident Galaxy, Kalinga Nagar,
Bhubaneswar-751003, Odisha, India

E-mail: info@blackeaglebooks.org
Website: www.blackeaglebooks.org

First International Edition Published by
BLACK EAGLE BOOKS, 2020

Mystery Of Leaves
by Prasanta Behera

Original Copyright © Prasanta Behera 2017, 2020
All rights reserved.

All rights reserved. No part of this publication may be reproduced, stored in a retrieval system, or transmitted, in any form or by any means, electronic, mechanical, photocopying, recording or otherwise without the prior permission of the publisher.

Editor: Simi (Sharmila) Acharya
Cover & Interior Design: Prabin Badhia
Illustrations: Prabin Badhia (www.prabinbadhia.com)
Haiku pencil sketch: Caleb Snodgrass

ISBN- 978-1-64560-140-1 (Paperback)
Library of Congress Control Number: 2020952094
Printed in United States of America

To all the women

who have shaped my life

Mother, Grandmother,

Wife, Sister, Friend,

Daughter

for their amazing

Inner Strength

Without your strength,

life could have been much different!

In memory of
100th birthday of my Grandfather
(1920 -2002)

Narrow road between rice fields

sitting behind Grandpa in motorcycle

winds caressing, feeling invincible.

Table Of Contents

A Journey 11

I

Sounds of Silence 15
The Emptiness 17
Silence 18
Sounds of Silence 19
Standing in the Desert Plain 21
Pilgrimage 23
Rainbow Circle 24
Fragrant Memories 26

II

Crossroads 27
Unexpected 29
Shadow and I 30
Between Lines 32
Unspoken Winds 34
Warrior of Light 35

III

Earth and Sky 37
Scent of Rain 39
Brook of Stevens Creek 41
The Ghosts of Moon 42
Shadows of Moon 44
Mountain Journey 45
Haikus 48

IV

Wave and Shores 53
Thoughts and Waves 55
The Untethered Boat... 56
Shadow in the Mirror 57
Unsettled Flicker 59
Falling Reflection.. 61
Wish 63

V

Mystery of Leaves... 65
Mystery of Leaves... 67
Mystery of Red Leaf 69
Mystery of Yellow Leaf 72
The Last Leaf 74

VI

Reminiscence 75
The Black Line... 77
The Lonely Chair 82
Finding Youth.. 86
Last Sunday 90
Reminiscence 92
Words from Swamiji 94
A small circle... 96
I write... 97
A Daughter for Life... 98
Before I am long gone... 100

A Journey

Before this journey, the thought of writing a poem or a short story was as remote as the farthest galaxy. But sometimes life puts us in a cross-road. I found myself standing in the middle of one of those lonely points in space in August 2015, from where endless roads stretched to the mountains, to the meadows, and vast deserts. There, gathering strength, reflecting, slowly I found myself chipping away the walls of emotions for a new journey. This may be a true reflective process or a middle age crisis, I do not know but like a stream, let it flow to the unknown. The journey started one afternoon on October 6, 2015, a shaky hand, overexposed heart, time and heartbeat stood still for a moment until few scribbled lines unlocking the past thoughts found its way.

Writing poems has been one part of this journey so far. I started hiking alone in the mountains, biking in the bay area roads early in the morning and writing a blog. It has been a newfound experience for me and in the process, I started reading regularly. I was influenced by Rabindranath Tagore and Paul Coelho in this process of self-discovery. This journey is not about reaching any mountain top or any destination, it is about reaching a place in the mountain to light a fire; a fire for oneself and a fire for someone else in need.

I do not think of myself as a poet or a writer, rather a traveler jotting some of my thoughts as part of my journey.

3 years later (2nd Edition)
When I re-read the poems, besides the editorial mistakes, I found many inconsistencies. So, I thought of updating the book and republishing it under a new banner for ease of access. I was hesitating but when I shared the idea to my friend Simi Acharya, she encouraged me to do so. She even volunteered to help edit and give feedback. I am deeply thankful for her encouragement and support in this journey. There was an urge to do major rewrite but sometimes the mistakes and inconsisten-

cies are there like flowers and thorns along with the emotions and feelings captured in the poems. So, I decided to do minor updates keeping the thoughts of the past captured in the fragmented words. I also took the opportunity to experiment some new ideas. Inspired by Baso's "The Narrow Road to Deep North" book, I decided to add some pencil pictures to some of the haikus with the help from Caleb Snodgrass, a pencil artist.

While discussing the poems of my second book ("Treasure Walks") with Prabin Badhia, an artist and a friend, he said why not collaborate on a few poems. I loved his expression paintings and always looked forward to collaborating sometime. So, I requested to interpret the four "Mystery of Leaves" poems in his own way. But slowly the collaboration grew to other poems and ideas too. The sketches are his interpretation. I loved his sketches; it pushes the imagination to a deeper self. I am deeply thankful for his collaboration and ideas. The cover page is his design and captures the essence of this book.

This book is an amalgamation of poetry and art, of friendship, and a journey of search within and a search of unspoken thoughts; to explore past and present; the strength to share and find a path to navigate forward; the scribbled lines has allowed me to explore myself.

Prasanta
2020

I
Sounds of Silence

The Emptiness

Sorrow of evening fog
lingers in the heart,
languishing in silence.
Roaming soul
in the hissing
meadow of emptiness,
searching for a
spot to shed tears.

October 2015

Silence

Silent universe, silent ocean
from silence, everything is born
AUM starts and ends with it.
Understand the river
the language of life
connects to the silent ocean.
Listen to the water
the water will speak to you.
Understand the ripples in silence.
Emptiness everywhere
atoms to universe, it is silent
Why are we afraid?
Let us embrace it.
It is the THE silence
the soul experiences at the end.
Let us understand the language of silence from the river
Let the river connect us to the ocean in silence
Let it help experience what we cannot in awake
At the end, we are just epochs in this silent world.

November 2015

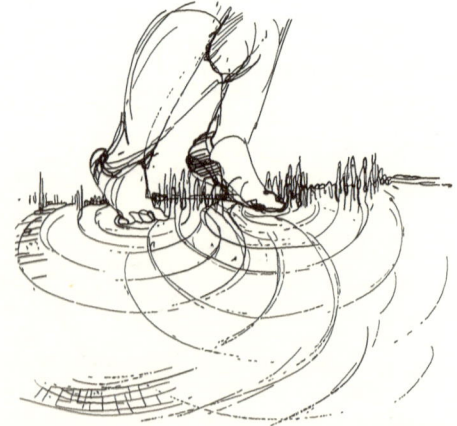

Sounds of Silence

I can hear the sound
the sound I was born with
the sound I carry in my heart
the sound of past
the sound of love
it is there, connected.
What was so close is now far
unfathomable deep gorge of silence
in between.

Listen to the deep
you can hear
the sound of silence
it is the same vibration
reminding of existence
reminding of joys
reminding of blessings
reminding of the life ahead
life which must be lived
life which must be experienced
life which must be traveled
life which must be shared.
Do not reminisce
of what you cannot hear
of what you cannot see
of what you cannot feel
it is there, it is eternal.

I do not feel stranded
in the deep ravine
I do not feel the need
to hear the sound;
It is in me
the same cosmic vibration
the same journey
in this unknown infinity.

August 21, 2016
(one year after the deep silence)

Standing in the Desert Plain

I found my temple
not in the corner of a busy street
not at the top of a mountain
not in a house of bricks and mortars
not in a building with a sign of OM
not in a building with a sign of Cross
not in a building with a sign of Crescent Moon
but I found in the midst of a desolate place
no paved roads lead to the place
no signs or emblems decorate
no buildings to signify its existence
a vast plain in the midst of a mountain.
Desert flowers scattered across
rocks playing hide and seek
a small stream sanctifying
gentle wind welcoming
Yes, I found my temple in the desert plains.

I do not need to pluck flowers
I do not need to carry water
I do not need the chanting book
I do not need to carry an incense
The desert flowers are the flowers
they come and go at the right time;
the holy water is in the streams flowing
nourishing and cleansing everything;
the scent of earth is the incense
for the heart to reminiscent till end;
there is no need for a chanting book
the wind is chanting the tunes eternal
no words required to understand the meaning;
I found my temple one evening
in the midst of mountain plains.

When I look all around
there are no pictures
there are no marble statues
there are no candle lights
the sky paints the pictures
the scattered stones are the statues
the night stars are the candles
everywhere I see the temple
no beginning or end;
I have found my temple
Now I just have to find the GOD
among the flowers, streams and mountains
listening to the chants from the winds.
Is there a need to find the GOD?
I am already realizing it
standing in the midst
the sky's still blue & orange
the flowers are blooming
the winds are still chanting,
one evening in this desert plains.

April 2017

Pilgrimage

Walk alone, walk at your own pace
do not worry about others passing by
find your own pace,
walk alone.

Pilgrimage is
not about places
not about people
not about soul
not about finding God
it is about you
it is about finding oneself
it is about finding one's own pace.

Walk in the dawn
walk in dusk
walk in the rain
walk alone;
experience the nature
observe small things
a tree leaf turning red
a small flower blooming
feel the vibrations from winds
it speaks to you
find your own vibration
harmonize it.
walk alone.
Walk alone in the rain
walk alone in the dark
walk alone in the early morning
but walk alone.
A lone.

November 2015

Rainbow Circle

Standing at the edge of Pacific Ocean
morning blue sky glittering the horizon,
I saw a silent wave merge into the ocean
never again to be a wave
never again distinguishable
never again alone
never again to be seen.

Cycles of sun and moon
pull and push the ocean waves,
alone I stand in the midst
between sunrise and sunset, I wait
for a message from the ocean.

Is it a coincidence or an unknown force
leading me to repeat the same journey
two years later on the same day when
the scattered ashes met the Pacific Ocean
this time, I am near the Atlantic Ocean,
a full circle, a journey with no ends.

I saw the rainbow veiled in mist
in this raging Niagara Falls for eyes to feast
a message of bliss engraved in the colors
but the heart understood the rainbow circle
what the eye sees is only a part
the other half is only for the heart,
an endless bliss from the ocean's depth.
When I saw the rainbow,
I understood
I have kept the promise
I have kept your hope
there is no wave anymore
you are the ocean now.

August 2017

Fragrant Memories

One day my son asked, "What is that rope for?
I have not seen it used as far as I remember."
An eight feet rope hangs in the trellis in the backyard
crossing between the post, North to South and back.
I said, "It was used when your grandma was here
Every day she would hang her sari(*) to dry in summer.
Use the power of the sun and wind instead of the dryer.
Now, it is just hanging, I have not bothered to remove it yet."

The answer was convincing enough;
my son moved on, no need to dig deeper.
Left alone in the trellis, I started to reminisce
l could imagine the colors of saris hanging
yellow colored sari one day, green the next
meticulously hanging until sunset.
Someday, it used to get stuck in between the ropes
she would call me to pull it down carefully.
I can still imagine the smell it carried
the fragrance of mother wrapped in between
it is hard to forget the breath that molded me.

I imagined the childhood days of long before
to avoid something scary or father's fury
hide behind her back, hands wrapped around
face buried in her sari for the moment to pass.
The smell of her fragrance and softness
protected me then as it does now in spirit;
the rope is empty, and it still hangs between the posts
she is no more; fragrant thoughts remain in the heart.

August 2020

(*) Sari - is a women's garment from the Indian subcontinent

II
Crossroads

Unexpected

What was a hope
was lost
What was gained
was unexpected.
Time stretched
and shrunk
in between .
What was to be said
was never said .
What was to be realized
never realized
between hope and loss
and loss and gain
life moved forward
reflection of past
blinking in distant
reminding of past
reminding of what was gained
a road ahead.

September 2016

Shadow and I

What I see is not me
what I am, I do not see
the shadow and I
traveling together
like quantum loops
in this mirage
of space and time.

Sometimes it is there
sometimes it is not
sometimes in the front
sometimes in the back
silent always
reminding of existence
reminding of non-existence
of light and darkness
between the cycles
of sun and moon.

The shadow is not me
yet I need it, reminds
the paths taken
the paths to be taken
silent as usual
playing hide and seek.
It is the shadow
who leaves me out of darkness
unmasking the reality
beneath the facade of
"What I am" and
"Who I am".

In the end, it is not me
but the shadow left behind
floating in the clouds
hovering with the wind
a reminiscence,
a blessing
to those left behind.
After the pouring rain
when the bright sun comes
there is no shadow
there is no "I"
merged in the cosmic vibration
woven in this quantum fabric
for eternity.

September 2016
(Tagore's "Stray Birds" influenced me for this poem).

Between Lines

Standing between
two imaginary lines
mist caressing
alone I am
in this vast plane
bounded
unfathomable road
what lies beyond
an oasis or a mirage
joy or pain
maybe all that wished for or not
invisible lines they are
I can feel it
I can sense it
there is an urge to
find what lies beyond
curious and foolish
the heart is.

Once crossed
there is no turning back
could leave a trail of joy
or a heavy cloud of sadness,
bounded by reality of existence
stranded in between, I am.
When I close my eyes, I see myself running
touching both lines, feeling its presence
noise becomes silence, light becomes dark
space becomes empty, lines become invisible
the lines that I was bounded by
have merged and so am I.

What I thought was lost
what was unknown
what was limiting
is gained, is known
is limitless
achieved in infinite.
in the end.

October 2016

Unspoken Winds

Unspoken words
unspoken thoughts
like desert wind
swirling and twisting
playing a dance
restless
turbulent
moments of calmness
in between
looking for an answer
In the unspoken winds.

A dark cold night
a beautiful sunrise
a mirage in between
the desert wind
the sand dune
intertwined in the journey
with epochs of existence
and deep long silence
inbetween.

Is it lost forever
like ghost towns
In the sand dunes
In this vastness of desert.
Galloping
galloping
a ghost rider, I am
In the sandstorm
Of unspoken winds.

October 2016

Warrior of Light

We are warriors of light
helping others pass the storm
enhancing the world everyday
we are warriors of light!

Veil of clouds surrounding
thoughts entrapped
blocking the light of hope
blurring the journey of life
look within, O Warriors of light
look within;
unknown paths
unknown is the end;
there is light within
find it, dance with it
completely merge with it
O Warriors of light.

Fight the ignorance
cherish the thoughts
find the light within
for a journey to be made
for love to be sprinkled
for hand to stretch beyond
wake up the warrior within
O Warriors of light!

November 2015

III
Earth and Sky

Scent of Rain

Spring afternoon
cloudy sky
gentle breeze
fluttering maple leaves
falling raindrops
seeds of life.

Watching from the window,
the rain and I, unattached
like talking without listening
like loving without feeling
like helping without loving
I wonder why this apathy
I search for the answers.
Rain
reminds of days of yore
dancing with you every summer
in the lands of my roots, long before.

O the dark clouds
the lightning and thunder
the anxious wait for rain drops
so that we can dance;
dance in the rain
to celebrate for future
we are farmers at heart!

Rain pours like falling stars
caressing the dusty veranda;
droplets kissing Mother Earth.
Feel the emotions
feel the droplets of rain
close your eyes

smell "the scent of rain".
Euphoric kids,
dancing, jumping, smelling
intoxicated by the fragrance
the union of land and
the blessing from heaven.

I cannot forget the feeling
I cannot forget the fragrance
it is inside me
reminding me of what we are
reminding of the land born.
It will be there
till I return to the land
to merge with the dust of my roots
to let the rain, bless again
to let kids, dance on them
to smell the "scent of rain."

May 2016

Brook of Stevens Creek

Biking alone in this narrow path
in the wee hours of a summer day
mind wanders like a banyan tree
with pebbles of thought from yesterday.
Sun rays play hide and seek
in the curved path between the trees,
the dew in golden grass shimmer
with the early morning sunrise.
The road is empty, the air is fresh
the sound of the pulsating water
over rocks and twigs mesh
uphill I go on bike catching my breath.

Thinking of the places far away
mountains of Peru, fountains of Rome
but the brook of Stevens creek is nearby
the tall redwood trees glorify
where I can be lost in thought
between the sound of the stream
and the touch of wind.

Let me take you to the brook
to touch the golden grass
to let the water cuddle your feet
to let you oscillate between shade and rays
to show you the pair of blue Jays
to the golden leaves caressing the creek
to the westerly winds hissing to the leaves
where you can you,
I can be I
together reflecting in hue.

July 2017

The Ghosts of Moon

O midsummer night moon
let me see your face
let me soak your rays of light
like dew drops caressing leaves,
we are connected
we are connected forever
but why do you hide from me;
what is on the other side?
The veil of the universe
shrouds in mystery;
what lies behind the facade,
what lies behind the brighter side?
Why are you afraid
to show the realm
do ghosts linger in them?

The moon says
"I can not change the path
I can not show the other side
but no ghosts linger in me.
What we see, not all there
what we feel, not all shared
what we tell, not all spoken
let my light sooth you
let it show you the path
to your journey in the
midsummer night
but trust me,
no ghosts linger in me!"

I look at the reflecting moon in the water
rays of moonlight shining in the ripples
there are no ghosts - why did I imagine?
Wake up, Wake up - the voice within say
ghosts are shadows of fear, one must conquer
The moon and the imagined ghosts
have helped in the journey of self!

December 2016, 2020

Shadows of Moon

The music of sorrow
from the gaps of life
lingers like a veil
reminding and uplifting
Life must continue
Life needs to exist

Like the moon
we must continue with
darkness of loss
on one side
blessings of light
on the other
Life must continue
between
light and dark
dreams and reality
past and future
like shadows
of the moon.

October 2016

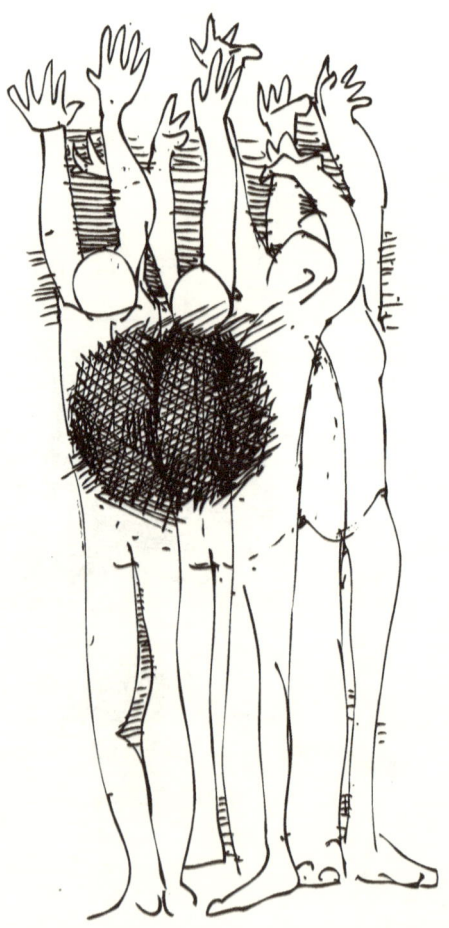

Mountain Journey

The mountain stands emotionless
watching the battle in its land
the victor go home
but the scar of death
lingers to the end.
The grounds soaked
of blood and sweat
the mountain is waiting
for the rain to lay the rest.
Victory pillars built
rituals performed
battlefield sanctified
the mountain is glorified
the victor lays the claim
the deceased lay in vain
but no one knows,
the mountain endures
haunting between
glory and pain.

History will note
the time and place
the victorious king
in this glorious place
the fallen kings
in this desolate place
but what about
the thousands of lives
lost in the battle
in this empty space?

The bodies have long gone
the withered victory column
stands alone
the flowers have bloomed
but no one knows
the scars beneath the stones.
Long ago the battle of Mahabharata
the winners were Pandavas(*)
the losers were Kaurvas (*)
but what about the thousands men
who died in the battlefield
who are they
do we know anything about them?
We remember the kings
winners or losers
but what about the ordinary men
there is no history etched for them.
Only the mountain remembers
the shadows of the fallen men
engraved in its stones until the end.

The mountain is beautiful
the mountain is glorious
lets us not raise victory pillars
to lay a claim in the valleys;
there is no victory in war
only a path forward
plant a tree instead of a tower
to remember the fallen
the mountain will bless us
for this token.

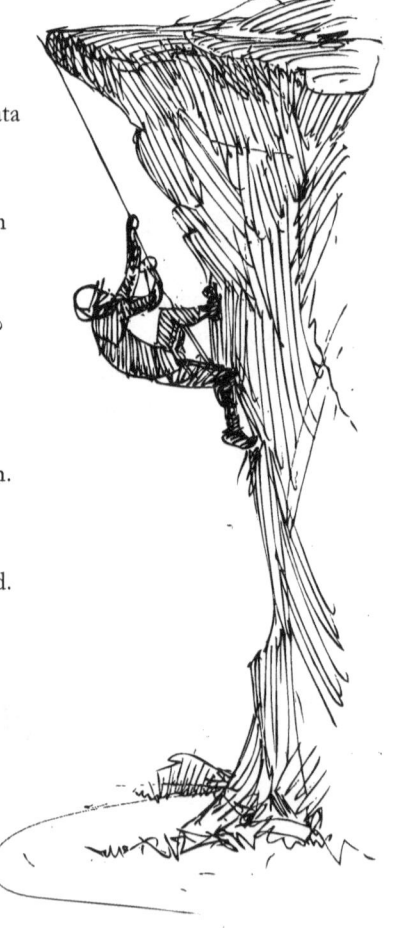

It is the same, deep inside our heart
battles are fought, wars are lost
but when we lay a claim
with a victory lap,
we dwell between
the same agony and pain
again and again.

March 2017
(*) "Pandavas" and "Kaurvas" were the legendary princes from Mahabharata, the great Indian epic.

Haikus

Caged birds fluttering
Under a Banyan Tree
Gold coin in the pocket
Morality beckons!

Alone at the beach
Masked by the fog
Waiting for sunrise
Flickering waves caresses

Starry dark night
crickets buzzing
Twinkling lantern light
Book in hand, alone.

Yellow mustard flower
soaking the western sun
Eyes got a glimpse
while zipping in the highway

Purple flower blossoming
Silent Buddha fountain
Quivering hummingbird sipping
Busy squirrel.

Blinds fluttering in middle of night
Eyes wide awake
Waiting for the sound of rain
Wife in deep sleep.

Lonely open road
Car and bike on both lanes
Trapped squirrel zigzagging
Aren't we all?

Barren maple tree
Awaiting birds to nest
Unfettered openness
Anxious mind.

Swallows air dancing
Over sprouted wheat plants
Tumbleweeds rolling
Nature's spectators

Village seems far
Mind running faster than legs
Paddy fields in between
Grandpa waiting.

Narrow road between rice fields
Sitting behind Grandpa
winds caressing
feeling invincible.

Setting sun in Death Valley
Shining hills like a painting
Covered in darkness now
Lost in emptiness.

Tethered balloon
southern winds
unable to escape
aren't we all.

Foggy mountain afar
red light in front
paused moment
light changes

Scattered fallen leaves
waiting a tempest
bug shelters under leaf

Dead deer on road
a cross from men
a red cone for deer
symbols of passing.

Three paths on the mountain
A signpost; a bird on top
I see paths, it sees none!

Flowing water yesterday
empty, exposed today
reveal like the creek.

Rows of lights twinkling
Reflecting hopes and dreams
Still darkness within

Orange horizon
Clouds underneath in motion
Observer I am.

Nov. 2015 - June 2017

IV
Wave and Shores

Thoughts and Waves

Thoughts like sea waves coming ashore
turbulent, anxiety abound …
not sure, where will it end
will it be on a welcoming beach
or meet a sorrowful end on the rocky coastline?

I await peacefully, anxiously caressing the sands
a gentle touch and the moments of silence
all that is needed … all that is needed.
fortune is on my side …
wide … accepting … warm …
magnanimous in awaiting.

What was a wave,
now is part of sea
merged but not lost.
Isn't that all we are,
cosmic dust?

The thoughts echoes in the heart
in the empty spaces between silent breaths
until the end...
Is there an end to a thought from the heart?

November 2015

The Untethered Boat

Life feels like an abyss
splintered road
untethered boat
drifting away
slowly vanishing in the sea.

Was the hope from the heart
was it pure like a raindrop
was it deep like an ocean
it was! ... it was!
I cannot blame the mountain
for not able to reach to the top
I cannot blame the flower
for not being able to smell the fragrance
I cannot blame the sun rays
for not being able to feel its warmth
I cannot blame the moon
for not being able to see the beauty.

If it was from the heart
if it was pure,
I must not suppress the thought of past
let it exist like the mountains of pacific ocean
let it exist like the soothing reflection of moon
let its fragrance exist in flowers of desert
let me help the drifting boat navigate the waves
let me help to its new destination
in the new journey of life;
I must, since the thought was
pure and from the heart.

October 2016

Shadow in the Mirror

What we see not all there is
behind the hidden fog
we carry the deepest secrets
brave are those souls
who speak through mirrors.

I see a shadow in the mirror
behind the layer of foggy veil
speaking to me,
a voice from the deep
I could hear not in ears but in heart
I could hear the words like a painted art
words wrinkled by time;
what I heard sank my heart
the stories of challenges and pain
the stories of falling back again
the invisible lines of tears
the lonely path traversed
in the lost time to be forgotten.

Droplets of fog streaks the mirror
emotions shared between shadow and I
I could not see myself in the mirror
blurred by guilt, crowded by emotions\
never before have I heard
of such pain so close by
never realized the dark spots
behind the shining moon.

Long ago the shadow
oblivious and silent
now it speaks in reflection
behind the foggy mirror.
I can not help the past
but I can help forward.
I wiped the mirror
let the droplets of sorrow fall
let me see the moon
let me feel connected
in infinity of reflection.

October 2016

Unsettled Flicker

Life moves forward
with a flicker in heart
deep inside hiding
struggling to stay alive
sometimes visible
sometimes invisible
sometimes excited
sometimes in pain
chained by the time
of past and present.

Time passes like a river
carrying the flicker in the heart
I hope to find the words
to make it calm
to be in peace.

Finally, I hear the sound
from the river
behind the mist of fog
faintly in a voice of known
I can understand it
I can feel it
I have been waiting
for that voice
for that sign
for those thoughts
to calm the flicker
to be in peace
to forge a new road.

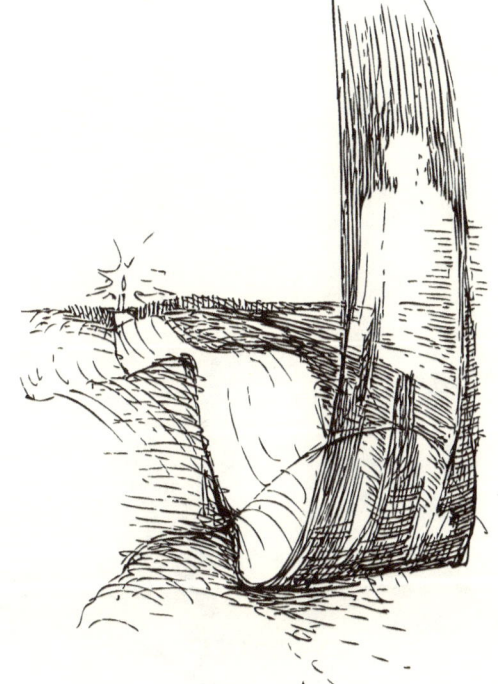

What was unsettled,
now in peace;
life feels richer, knowing,
the voices within;
carrying the flicker
of past in the heart,
I forged ahead feather light
knowing well, it is still there.

July 2016

Falling Reflection

We fall often to be picked by someone
that has not changed from the day we were born
as a child, we do not question
but as an adult, we surround it by reasoning
mind goes in circles looking for a clue
but we know deep inside, there is none to choose.
A dream of shadows and light
a stretched hand in the midst
mist of fog, birds in flight
wake up O' fallen knight!

Walking across the narrow trail
in the park below the Black mountain
the racing mind calms anew.
thoughts of yesterday seems afar
the reasons, the whys and why nots
of falling again feels like a shooting star.
I see a pond with a pier in the midst
few birds enjoying the evening mist
the ripples in pond enjoying the breeze
the seaweed dancing underneath
reminds of the days long before
when falling and getting up again was not a chore.

The seaweed dancing with the ripples
glancing sun piercing through the mist
a lonely boat docked at the pier
a pair of ducks gliding the waters
a surge of unbridled spirit in the air,
I bent down from the pier to take a picture
forgetting the shadow of the soul sitting across.
As I get closer, my eyeglasses fall in the water
quickly I try to catch
Alas! I am no match
the glasses keep falling
I feel I am also falling with it
to the entangled labyrinth of the deep.

The shadow sitting across laughs at my desperation
I do not know why; I start to laugh with realization
at my own foolishness with emotions
the dreamer voice of the deep says
laugh loud that the ripple can carry with it
laugh loud so that the birds can hear it
like the eyeglasses, we all fall into abyss
what we all need is shadow to laugh with it
O dreamer of shadows and light!

May 2017

Wish

You said, "I wish
If I could go to the mountains like you
If I could be with nature alone
If I could see the skypilot flowers
If I could hear the birds fluttering
But I am not yet ready to make it happen
but someday, I wish - I can."

I said, "I also wish
If I could hike in the mountains of Himalayas
If I could roam in the steppes of Patagonia
If I could to travel in the deserts between mirages
If I could make pilgrimages in search of myself
someday I wish, I can do all
beyond reach, some will remain a wish
but I know, I will keep on trying."

Every time I hike the mountains
you see every flower that I see
you hear every bird singing that I hear
you see the sunrise as I do
you get layered in fog as I do
you feel the wind as I do
you are there in spirit traveling
you may have wishes, unknown to me
I only know about this
you can experience your wish
If you choose, framed by my journeys
I walk alone in search of mine.

September 2020

V
Mystery of Leaves

Mystery of Leaves

Sitting alone in a cafe in the afternoon
sun breathing through the clouds
the aroma of warm coffee
leaves falling from trees
a gentle breeze...
fluttering book pages
leaves dancing with the wind
eyes wanders...
not sure what it is looking for.

Suddenly, I see her
sitting across by herself
deep blue eyes
eyes that have a mystery behind it
eyes that have a deep sorrow
eyes with light like no other.
I wonder how that can be;
tears and beaming light together?
The falling leaves
dressing the earth like a mosaic.
The evening sun peeking
creating patterns of light and shade
the gentle breeze whispering to me
as if it wants to say something.

The aroma of coffee
navigating like a messenger
she is oblivious to all these
lost in thought.
Time passes by…
suddenly she gathers her thoughts
pauses a bit
picks two leaves
one red and one yellow.
stares at them for a while
as if they are speaking to her.

She looks around
our eyes meet for a split second
feels like looking far into deep blue ocean
unknown… mysterious…
she smiles back like a dew falling from a folded leaf
I close my eyes for a moment
she is gone with the red leaf on my table…

I ponder about the red leaf
perhaps the labyrinth of lines tells the story
the darker shadows she is leaving behind
moving on with the brighter yellow leaf.
not sure why it was me
not sure why it was the red leaf
not sure what the leaf is saying.
I put the red leaf in my book
hoping that our paths will cross again
the mystery of the red leaf will haunt me till then.

December 2015

Mystery of Red Leaf

Barren trees awaiting the spring
transitioning between old and new
rain and cold testing the spirit.
sitting near fireplace struggling
what to read on this cold evening.

Flipping through a book, I see the red leaf
awakens the forgotten memory,
like lightning, mind starts to
illuminate the forgotten.
Why did she give me the red leaf?

Lost thoughts spring forward
looking for answers in the
labyrinth of possibilities
but none makes sense.

Night turns to day
what was lost before
remains unanswered now.

The universe works in mysterious ways
when you truly seek it.
While strolling in the park one evening
I saw her again, sitting on a bench alone
full of jest with the unforgettable smile
same deep blue eyes.

Mind and heart struggle
between emotions and reasoning
With enough strength, I approached her
questions that have haunted me for a long time.
Why did she give me the red leaf?

She sighs for a moment, closed her eyes
recollecting the past.
Only birds seem to know the chasm
of silence and waiting.

Finally, I hear her voice, sweet but deep
"When I met you, the past was haunting me
struggling to move forward in life.
The red leaf helped me answer
gave me strength to move forward.
So I only walked out with the yellow leaf
leaving the red one for you".
Why me?

"When I saw you, you seemed to be lost
like a wounded warrior, a path yet to be discovered.
I hoped you could find your answers like me
in the labyrinth of the leaf.
Red color symbolizes courage and passion
gives strength to find paths unseen;
what you may have thought as lost
was always there before "
I was astounded by what she observed in me.
How did she?

She opened the purse and took out
the yellow leaf from a folded page
hands me the leaf, "You are ready for it now..
Look at the lines, it tells the story
She starts walking slowly
slowly fading away…

An uncanny silence piercing through
thoughts struggling to settle
the "fog of unknown" still lingering.
Eye look towards the path she went
heart sinks. I may never see her again.
I am not alone, on this journey now.

Evening chill slowly settles in
bringing the veil of emptiness within.
I picked up the yellow leaf
carefully placed, answers lie within
this folded page.
I start thinking of the new journey
a smile for her and questions for me!

February 2016

Mystery of Yellow Leaf

Spring gives way to summer
yellow golden grass shimmers the landscape.
The yellow color brings back memories
to the last riddle of the journey,
to be discovered in the in
the yellow leaf.
The thoughts, the questions
the answers hidden within.

Is this real or a dream
or a naked experience
in search of the journey?
I am here.
I am here on this journey.
Everyone is here too
contained in this labyrinth
interconnected but invisible.

The veins in the leaf tells about our souls
influencing others like gravity
in this fabric of dream and reality
shadows we all are.

Who was she?
Who was the blessed soul?
She is a hervuta (*),
a soul deeply connected
in real and in dream
from past to eternity,
a soul not part of destiny
but part of the journey.

What was mysterious
what was unknown
what ached the heart
what troubled the mind
what was incomplete
is now known
is now complete.
A hevruta indeed;
unknown yet connected
in dream and reality.

Like an ocean, I feel the depth
the turbulence and calmness.
The journey is not complete
and it may not be;
but I know the path now
a path revealed in the yellow leaf.
The quest is not finding a path
The quest is not to find an answer
The quest is to find the havruta(*)
who can walk along the path to
to make the journey complete!

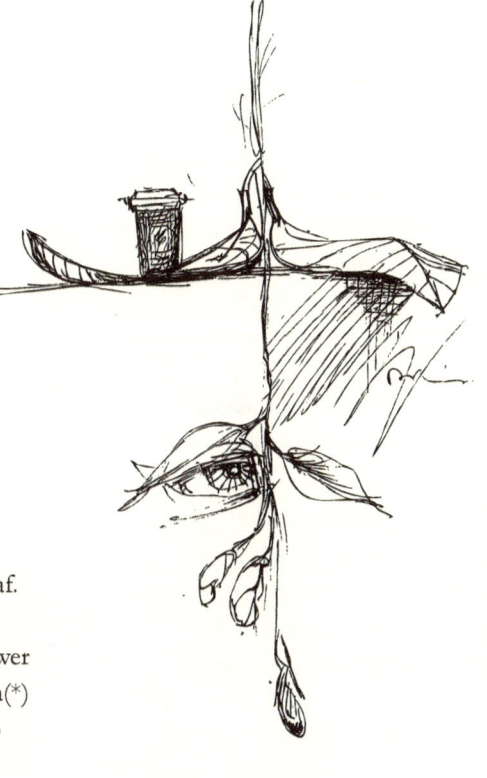

(*) Hevruta (a yiddish word) is someone who pushes and challenges you, someone who gives you the opportunity to complete yourself.

July 2016

The Last Leaf

The splendor of fall
ending slowly after all.
The leaves are almost gone
but not for long.
Like the tree waiting
for the last leaf to fall,
so am I with the yellow leaf
waiting to let go after all,
a mystery revealed;
a journey answered.

The realized and unrealized forces
clashing at the ocean shore;
in one moment, you hear the turbulent waves
with shadows of thoughts coming ashore,
in the next, the calmness of water
spreading the ocean beach soothing the amber
reminding of what was lost and there now
reminding of what was experienced and unexperienced
reminding all what meant-to-be and not-to-be
reminding for the journey taken and yet to take
reminding for the time spent and emptiness.

Like the tree,
let the last leaf fall.
Let me be the wave
let me carry the yellow leaf to the ocean
carrying all thoughts and emotions
etched in the labyrinth of this yellow leaf
be lost forever in depths the ocean
and let this wave merge along with it.

February 2017

VI
Reminiscence

The Black Line

The shadow of moon ripples in the pond
flickering lights playing hide and seek
the barren mountain stands tall
a nestled village layered in fog.
The black line slithers on the mountain slope
like a big snake crawled before
children close their eyes, adults try to rush
when they cross the mountain slope.
Every line has a story
may it be in the sand or on the leaves;
in the mind or on the face
each line has a story to be told.

The black line on the mountain
has a story; a story which
gives chills to children,
reminds the adults of the valor;
makes the mountain proud.
It was on this slope
the mighty warrior Bhima(*)
killed the the big black slithering snake
on a starless night;
saving the village from misery.

The slithering lines
the mark of severed head
the giant steps of Bhima
it feels real, it feels recent.
The adults feel blessed
the children are in awe
touching and feeling
the black line in the mountain slope

dreaming ... acting...
like how it happened not so long before.

It a story we all keep in heart
growing up, villagers we all are.
We are the dust of the mountain
we are its reflection.
One day we will be a dust
and so, will be the mountain
but until then
the mountain has the story
the mountain sees everything
the mountain feels everything
we are the dust of the mountain.

II

The black line stands still
time has not altered it
darkness has not hidden it
sunlight has not blurred it
it is there reminding
to the old and the new
keeping story alive
keepin the mystery intact
generation to generation.

III

I see a small girl
standing at the front door
hair uncombed
tattered clothes;
a ring in the nose

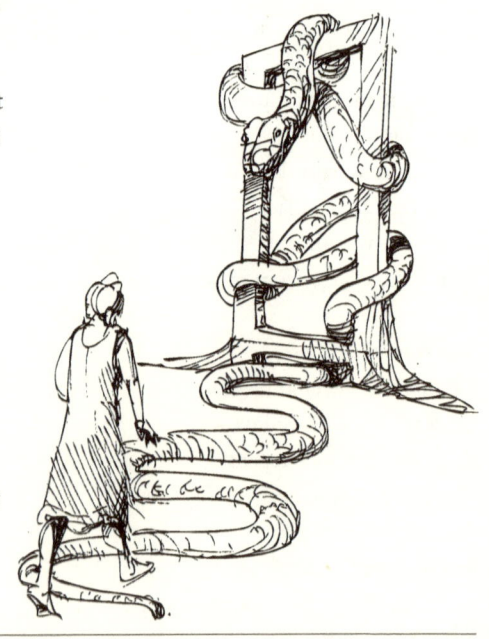

a basket in hand
a smile like a rose
standing at the door frame
sun behind
shadow in-front.

She is waiting
she calls out once;
waits for some time, calls again
everyone is listening yet ignoring.
She sighs back with a grin
leaning to the door frame;
sun shining from behind
the long shadow across the door,
she wants to cross the door
hesitates, waits again …

The shadow is growing longer
but her smile has not withered
I asked her to come in
leave the basket in the corner.
She hesitates and takes a step
withdraws back to her old sigh.
Why is she not crossing the door?
I can not understand.
May be she is too shy, may be unsure
I ask her again to make sure.

She hesitates a bit, starts to step inside
but I hear a yelling afar
"Do not come in
stay where you are."
The same voice explains
"she can not come in

she is of lower caste
she can not come in
young master
a line separates us".
I don't understand
because like her,
I am a young man.
But I did not protest
what a shame!

IV

Decades have passed
the mountain is still there
the black line is still there
the fazed picture of the girl
standing at the door
echoing till today.
Where was the Bhima
the mighty warrior in me
when I needed it
to smash that door
to free the barriers within
Where was the Bhima in me
when I needed it!
But it is not late,
awake the Bhima inside
let him cut the black snake
as he did before in mountains
let him smash the door
let the young girl cross the door
Why do we have doors which we cannot cross
Why do we have doors, we cannot cross?

V

The mountain is still there
the black line is still visible
but tears roll in slopes of mountain
for the lines of division
we all created
lines of caste
lines of religion
lines of nationality
lines of color.

The mountain is crying
It can not understand
why we have lines
between the shadow and I
the shadow can cross
but not I
What is the difference?
We are the dust of mountains
we are the its reflection
we both have black lines.
Let us awake the Bhima
from deep inside
to make us all free from
the lines , the doors
which keeps us aside.
Why do we need lines?
Why do we need doors?
break those to make a difference.
I should. I must.

November2016

(*) "Bhima" is the legendary prince from Mahabharata, the great Indian epic.
He is known for his strength and might.

The Lonely Chair

I am the chair
in the center of the veranda
made of wood, heavy as a bull
arms wide like an elephant trunk
comfortable like a mother's lap
welcoming like the blue sky
from dawn to dusk to dawn;
I am the chair.

I am that lonely chair
waiting for someone
waiting for the one who
makes me feel like a king's chair
taps my handle like a tabla player
hums like a farmer waiting for rains
I have been waiting for him since morning.

Where is that tall man
with cotton white clothes
arms strong like a bull
chest wide as the mountain
sits hours with me
humming, tapping
waiting for someone
just like I am waiting
for him.

The joy he gets when he sees the child
fiddling his legs to welcome home
unable to sit still, anxious moments.
It feels like a mountain
waiting for the clouds to meet

a beautiful sight indeed
a beautiful sight indeed!
He does not want to let go
puts the child in my wide arm
for both him and I to enjoy.
Oh! the times we spent
the laughter, the silence and
everything in between.

Years have gone by
I have not seen him
many came and sat on me
stood on top me
but I do not feel a thing
they could be living or dead
they could be rich or poor
they could be men or women
I can not feel a thing
I am alone unconnected
unloved in this lonely place
waiting and waiting for
one who knows me.

I can see the cracks in my arms
I can see the faded colors
I can hear the squeaks
time has passed by waiting for him
reliving the memory of
what felt like yesterday
I am still waiting for him.

I find myself alone
in the corner
covered in darkness.
no one is sitting on me
no one is touching me
years have gone by.
I have been replaced
by a white plastic chair
a chair of no character.
Oh what a pity! What a pity!

Suddenly
I feel the tickle
I feel the same sensation
I feel the same feeling
I feel the same tapping rhythm
Is he back, enjoying me again!
It feels different
not the same touch
not the same strength
not the same tune
not the same majestic posture
but I know the sensation
I can feel it!
But alas, it is not him
the child of yesteryears now a man
echoing shadows of the one I miss.

I enjoy a few moments of the old glory.
It is not the same!
It is not the same!
I will wait for him
in this dark corner
let the shadows befriend me
let the cobwebs hug me
let the dust comfort me
I will be vigil
I wait for him.
in this dark corner
till the end of me.

August 2016
Whenever I used to go to my village, my grandfather was always sitting in a big heavy chair in the front porch waiting and waiting. Now the chair has been empty and will be empty till the end)

Finding Youth

Finally, the rain gods have visited us
sending dark clouds for many days
soothing this drought mired land.
The creeks are full
the earth is blessed
the clouds are still hovering over
but today, there is no rain
you feel the joy, you feel the energy
let us go to the mountains
for a ray of sun
for a breath of fresh air
for the lonely walk
but why am I rushing
when the trees look beautiful
when the flowers are peeking
and the air is fresh.

Like the bikers and walkers
I am also walking and running
in this narrow path we all share.
A puddle in the midst, a decision in-front
how to circumvent it and go to the mountain
as fast as I can.
But not to this little girl
who sees the puddle of water
runs forward in excitement
she crisscrosses it back and forth
with arms open and wide
circles around again and again
like the swan with pride.
Patient father stands still
imagining of his youth
a rainbow on a cloudy day.

II

"Cheers to the youth"
we raise our wine glasses
men and women in the middle years
but what is that "youth" we are craving for
is it the look we have or pretend
or is it the ideas or idealism we intend
What binds me to my youth
I do not understand.
Where is the youth I left behind
I lament deep inside
time has moved it far away
behind the fog of yesterday
but what I lament deep inside
hidden in the deep corner it is there
needs some light, to come outside.

III

Of all the crazy things that I do
What is the thing which
reminds of my yonder years
what was innocent at that time
is now is no more
a mirror of fog lay in front
let me find that thing which
connects to my yonder years
let me find that place
where I do not go around
like the little girl in the puddle.
I need to solve this riddle.

"You are weird", says my inner voice
when I rumbled through the pile of leaves
scattered in heaps small and big,
walk through them every fall.
The red and yellow fallen leaves
scattered across the path
why do you walk through them
O friend, when you can go around them.
I do not know why I do it
walking over the leaves
listening to the crackling sound
in this hazy evening sunlight.

Walking in the leaves reminds
of yonder years
when I use to run around
in the rice fields after the crop
spreading hands across like a bird
touching every stalk on the path
going in a zigzag, connecting to earth.

IV

Of all the things of youth
I lament
Of all the crazy things
I still do
I did not know
deep in the corner of my heart
a flicker of youth I hold inside.
It is the thing I do, alone or otherwise
What I had experienced in the rice fields
long ago, I find it in fallen leaves now
deep in the pile of hays and leaves
I find myself buried inside.

The little girl showed me
what I could not connect before
the thread of youth
from the yonder years
which I relive in every Fall.

February 2017

Last Sunday

I ate a bug last Sunday
biking uphill with morning sun rays.
between the huff and puff
one small fly went straight right up,
I could not catch it fast enough.
Before I know it, another landed
right inside my mouth like a jet
I did not have time to let.

It reminds me the rainy days of summer
in my village where fields, mountains are friends
and the house where the day ends.
Sitting in rows for dinner in the courtyard
rain dripping in spurs
three dingy lanterns lighting
circling them hordes of flies fighting.
When the winds and rain blow the light away
some of those flies lands on our food anyway
Grandma tells us to eat in hurry
or else "you will be eating bugs in your curry."
I am sure I ate few bugs no matter how fast I ate
It was not all that bad as far as I can say.

I told my son about what I did last Sunday
"You are weird dad", he said in a funny way
I also told my wife about it
"You behave younger than your son day by day.
I do not know what crazy things you will do next."
Now that I wrote a small poem about it
all my friends will say
"Hmm! he is getting weirder day by day
what strange things he will try next",
but I am sure when I tell it to my young nephews and nieces,
they will say, "Awesome! does it taste like sour candy!"

August 2017
(Dedicated to my young nieces and nephews who visit each summer, we have lots of fun making "Oompa-Loompa" songs and drinking T-pumps!)

Reminiscence

Why do I reminisce
the land where I was born?
Is it the mountains, the rivers
the rice fields or the dust in the road.
What beacons thee?
I do not know.
Here in this new land
that I live now
the mountains are bigger
roads are cleaner
orchards are bountiful
but the heart lingers away
to the dusty road
of yesteryears.

What beacons thee
the nostalgia of yesteryears
to smell the petrichor again?
Time turned tides
young turned old
memories of old
engraved in stones
in that dusty road
needs to be retold.
The shadows of the past
haunting the deep
to find a spot in hearts keep
to safely pass the thread of journey
to ask a question of destiny
"Where will your stone rest?"
That's the question
lingers in the heart

reminding of yesteryears
to carve the stone
as the time come near.

Like the roots of banyan tree
we need to grow
adventures we all are
we need to sow.
It is in the new land
I need to lay my stone,
like my forbearers
who carved the stones for
the dusty road walked for years
will keep lingering in the heart
a new stone, a new path
a new land, adventure begins!

April 2017

Words from Swamiji

We bereaved for a friend over zoom
stuck at home due to COVID19;
everyone shared their memories one by one
we were a tribe finding solace in words
on the tenth day, a learned Swami came
he chanted Vedic mantras in Sanskrit
explained its meaning line by line;
Of Life and Death
Of Impermanence
Of True Self
like a sponge and a rock, I oscillated
some words got absorbed
most went over the head.

Just as Swami finished his explanation
the zoom chat window bust into action
"Excellent talk Swamiji", one said
"Beautiful words Swamiji", said another
I did not say anything … I was still reflecting.
Are words like flowers measured in beauty?
Unlike the flowers of the garden, a momentary look,
a sniff, beauty measured and time elapses.
Are the words Swamiji spoke beautiful that way?
I could not say for sure what truly meant to me
only a few words I could hang on from that moment
my ignorance requires more time and thought,
I will not say anything for now.

Few weeks passed since the Swamiji's lecture
only two words I still remember
it resonates in the empty spaces;
oscillating between the two, searching for oneself
Now, I thank the Swamiji for his words
and the beautiful soul that got us connected
between mind's inference and the rest of the spaces
the enveloped beauty of Self, reflected.

May 2020

A small circle

Between cup of tea and chit-chats
I hear murmurs in passing
who got invited and who did not
to the events in the past and ones coming by
weddings, anniversary, milestone birthdays
meetings with the political leaders and influencers
I used to fall in that trap once
but no more.

I created a circle, a very small circle
inside which I am sure to get invited always
no doubt - no pretension - no anxiety
I have been happy since then
It is a very small circle
I am the only one inside
I invited myself to exist
I invited myself to Life, the best party.

February 2020

I write

I write poems on what you may have said
I write poems on thoughts you may have shared
I write poems on things you do in silence
I write poems on vibrations unnoticed
I scribble many; only a few get published.

When you read the poems printed later
You say, "You are observing too much."
I say, "Like the cascading flow from a waterfall,
your thoughts touch like drops of water
a calmness vibrates as I navigate closer;
paddling the boat in the whirlpool of emotions
I try harder in the midst of mist of unknown;
I hang on to the droplets of water like pearls
some of those become poems, many remains
I am just a traveler observing you in silence."

The words are mine but the thoughts are yours.
I write, knowing full well you are the poet in causation
lost in thoughts, I just capture few words in oscillation
I may write poems on what you will say
I may write poems on thoughts to be shared
I may write poems on things you will do in silence
I may write poems on vibrations experienced
I write but I am not a poet.

October 2020

A Daughter for Life

The gentle touch
curious eyes
the sleepy sighs
fitting in two palms
fatherhood begins with tears in the eyes.

The little flower blossoming
the gentle kisses in the cheek
the nibbling of ears
the sound of trinkets
I feel blessed that I have a daughter.

The sleepy head on shoulders
the occasional hug
the dancing footsteps
the sound of your sweet voice
makes life experiences beautiful.

The drive to Berkeley
the occasional talk
the sound of Odissi(*) music
the rhythm of your dance
mesmerizing feeling of joy like never before;
the challenges for fatherhood vanish at that moment.
The emptiness when you left for college
the occasional visit to home
always eagerly waiting
for the opening sound of the garage door...
fatherhood is like a river
ready to give a hug and lift you up.

Time is moving forward
the little girl turning into a young woman
the young daughter turning into a friend
the cactus birthday present
the "you are awesome too Dad" text
keeps older memories alive.
Many times, I feel I want to hold that
little girl in my arms again
and let her know how blessed I am.

Like a branch of a tree, you will explore the sun
establish your path, a journey on your own
but remember to connect to the root
from where you have grown.

A time will come, my body will become frail
It was a mother who gave birth to me to start the journey
It will be a daughter who will see me through till the end
I am glad I have a daughter!

January 2016
(*) "Odissi" is a type of Indian classical dance style

Before I am long gone

I lay in a casket with flowers covered
face calm, eyes closed, motionless
everyone is there
but I am long gone!

The tears roll in, the voice chokes
many speak of my loving spirit
magnanimity and friendship.
It may be true and may not be at all
does it matter, I am long gone!
Why do we say things when it does not matter
shouldn't they say before I am long gone?

So, I decided to throw a surprise party
before I am long gone;
everyone came
everyone asked what's the occasion
I told them it is my pre funeral party
everyone is shocked;
thought must be a bad joke
but I tell them, this is the ultimate truth
better to know it before I am long gone!

You have the chance to tell me what you think
tell the truth of friendship
tell truth of fatherhood
tell the truth about our love
tell the truth.
Let me soak in and understand

one by one started speaking
of things, I have done right and wrong
I oscillate between light and dark
would they have said this
when I am long gone!

Suddenly someone seating in the dark corner
stands up and comes forward
everyone looks at her as she speaks in slow
she says, "Yes, he has all the human fallacies...
but he has lit the fire for me when I needed most
he has shown me the path to move forward
he has shown me the path when I needed most"
I listened, not sure what I did for her
can not find the answer now...
I feel good, at least I have helped one soul
before I am long gone!

When the time comes
let my funeral be in silence
let my ashes float in pacific ocean
let there be sounds of antiquity
let there be joy for meeting eternity
Yes, I am long gone!

(Moon of the Falling Leaves 2015)

Prasanta Behera lives in California, USA. A hiker and biker, dabbling in poetry. This is his first book, now republished. His second poetry book "Treasure Walks" was published in July, 2020.

www.ingramcontent.com/pod-product-compliance
Lightning Source LLC
Chambersburg PA
CBHW021128080526
44587CB00012B/1176